Cultivating a Healing Home
 in the midst of the stress and worry of young motherhood
Rachael Belle Bomsta
ISBN 9798718280319

To my husband Danny. We will never have the perfect healing home we want this side of heaven, but we do have a imperfectly perfect home. You are my inspiration to keep moving forward. I love you and this home we have created.

Contents.

Contents.

Your invitation

You are about ready to go on a twenty-one adventure. Twenty-one days diving into motherhood through the lens of your role as a healing mother and the worries and fears that can strike us. Are you ready?

The first week we are going to tackle what a healing home looks like. Where does it start? Who builds a healing home? What does surrender have to do with it? What does gratitude have to do with our homes? And what happens when the fears of motherhood strike and your healing home seems distant?

The second week we are diving into when anxiety strikes our motherhood. We all have fears. Anxiety is a staple among mothers. Yet the healing power of the Gospel of Jesus Christ can transform our fear, worry, and anxiety as we lay our worries at the foot of the cross.

The third week is when everything is laid out on the open and we fully explore the expectations of being a woman of <u>surrender.</u> What does it mean to be a godly women of surrender? It's time to let Jesus be the ultimate builder of our homes as we surrender our entire family, home, and life to him.

A Healing Home

Unless the Lord builds the house,
those who build it labor in vain.
Unless the Lord watches over the city,
the watchman stays awake in vain.
Psalm 127:1 ESV

Day 1
<u>*Who Builds the Home?*</u>

Unless the Lord builds the house,
those who build it labor in vain.
Unless the Lord watches over the city,
the watchman stays awake in vain.
Psalm 127:1 ESV

I was up again with crying babies. I knew my alarm clock would go off at 2:50 am and I would have a limited amount of time to do my work before my children would be up for the day. It was 1:30am. Exhaustion spilled from my eyes in the form of wet, hot, overwhelmed tears. I cuddled my baby and laid him down again in his crib.

I can't do this anymore. Jesus, I can't do this anymore.

Have you ever been there? Chances are if you are a mother, you too have experienced the early morning cries of your baby. They wrench at your heart for two reasons.

First, you just want to go fix everything that is causing your sweet child discomfort. Second, you desperately want the cries to stop. You are tired, exhausted, stressed, worried, and at your end.

Dear mama, you are at a place of surrender, and it is time to look at your emotions through the lens of Jesus and taste the sweet surrender of Gospel freedom.

Surrender is a beautiful thing. It is that moment in time where you are confident that you no longer can function under the rule of your own sinful heart.

One of my greatest desires as a wife and mom on this side of eternity is to create a healing space, a healing home for my children to grow. Perhaps you desire a similar thing. You do not want your children to be entrenched, pushed and pulled by the evils of this world.

A healing home is a space that protects and nourishes little ones and grown ones from the destruction of the world.

...the whole world lies in the power of the evil one.
1 John 5:19 ESV

Our homes just may be the only safe haven that our children, husband, and those that enter our home may experience that day. Is your home a place of healing, or is it a byproduct of an evil world?

But do not worry dear mama, it is not your job to build it. Remember, you are exhausted. I see you at your end pulling up your 'big girl undies' and white knuckling it through motherhood.

Read again Psalm 127:1. Are you building in vain, or is the Lord building your home? All your efforts are for nothing, if the Lord is not the one building it.

Surrender. Surrender your home, your life, your motherhood to Jesus. Your healing home is about to begin.

Day 2
<u>The Healing Place of Imperfection</u>

You shall be careful therefore to do as the Lord your God has commanded you. You shall not turn aside to the right hand or to the left. You shall walk in all the way that the Lord your God has commanded you, that you may live, and that it may go well with you, and that you may live long in the land that you shall possess.
Deuteronomy 5:32-33 ESV

It had been a terrible day. Nothing went according to plan. I was dealing with it alright on the surface, but inside my heart was miserable. I was walking from the dining room into my messy kitchen trying to get dinner on the table when my toddler completely wreaked me.

"Mama, I liked today. I like playing with you."

Inside my heart, mind, and soul went topsy turvy . *How could have he liked today?! Nothing went right!*

It was in that moment that God nudged my heart and mind. My perception was not the same as my toddler's. He looked out through the innocent eyes of a child. What I saw was the mess, unruliness, and dysfunction. What he saw was a day filled with adventure. He saw a mama that played with him, a brother that laughed, and a home that was his kingdom.

That moment broke me and a word rang through my head for the next few days: **faithfulness.** God does not call us to perfection. He calls us to faithfulness. As mamas we are to be faithful to our calling, to our mission, and to our savior, Jesus.

When the Israelites received the 10 Commandments they were reminded not to turn aside to the right or the left. What was the result if they did not turn aside? Verse 33 explains that the result was that it would *'go well with you.'* Their faithfulness to the commandments of the Lord led to their wellbeing.

Is it a stretch to assume that we can reap the same benefits when we are faithful to our calling as a parent? I do not think so. Does that mean that faithfulness leads to perfection. No, and the beauty of that is that Jesus' mercy and grace now can step into our imperfect faithfulness and redeem our motherhood journey.

Yes, we are called to be faithful to our mothering, but our faithfulness is anchored in the grace of Jesus.
For it is by grace you have been saved, through faith—and this is not from yourselves, it is the gift of God— not by works, so that no one can boast.
Ephesians 2:8-9 NIV

What broke me that day when my toddler saw our day through a different lens, was that my imperfection as a mama was still enough because of the grace of Jesus stepping in to redeem what I thought was lost.

Be faithful, mama, and remember that Jesus is your anchor.

Day 3
<u>Burnt Up</u>

Every man's work shall be made manifest: for the day shall declare it,
because it shall be revealed by fire; and the fire shall try every man's
work of what sort it is. If any man's work abide which he hath built
thereupon, he shall receive a reward. If any man's work shall be burned,
he shall suffer loss: but he himself shall be saved; yet so as by fire.
1 Corinthians 3:12-15 NLT

I have a habit of starting lots of DIY home projects. Creating
more beautiful spaces is something that drives me, relaxes
me, and inspires me. I love looking at a cupboard and thinking
about how to white wash or paint it to create a more
beautiful area. Shopping at my local Menards or Home Depot
gets me all fired up with anticipation of my next project.
Power tools simply make me happy! Yet only recently have I
realized that this form of 'self-care' is also destructive.

How is creating beauty in my home destructive? Because I
become obsessive. There have been more DIY projects than I
can count where the project takes over my day and my
children are left playing by themselves.

Often my kids love participating with me in these projects.
They help measure, paint, and all their play tools end up
taking over the DIY space. It can be a precious time, but also
a self-centered time.

Self-care is essential to our sanity, but the danger of self care
is letting it become self-centered.

1 Corinthians 3:12-15 reminds me that my works on this earth will burn up. My works will be made manifest. Manifest simply means *'clear or obvious to the mind.'*

Although I have no intention of stopping my crazy DIY obsession, I do need to rethink its significance in my life. Is the DIY project more important or is the training and precious time with my kids while I am doing the project more important?

My new accent wall in my master bathroom will someday disintegrate and decay, but the moments with my children working side by side possibly has eternal implications.

How about you, what is something in your life that needs some adjustments? Your hobbies are important. They are what make you who you are! But how will they be made manifest in eternity? Do not let the good things in life become more important than the best things in life. It may just have eternal consequences.

Day 4
<u>Grateful for a Shed</u>

Oh give thanks to the Lord, for he is good;
for his steadfast love endures forever!
I Chronicles 16:34 ESV

The view from my first home was beautiful. We overlooked a rolling field that almost constantly had a slight breeze. There was a huge oak tree that framed the view with its towering branches. A small swing gave evidence to the breeze and created a picturesque setting. Plum trees danced with blossoms during the early Spring. Wildflowers grew from the ditches in the summer. Leaves cascaded throughout the autumn months, and winter left its mark by intricate frost and snow. It was beautiful.

However.

By contrast, looking into my driveway there was the most pathetic shed ever. Its appearance was shaggy, horrid, and I was disgusted by its rot. The shed was pieced together with various mismatched materials, it leaned to one side, the plywood bloated with age, the roofed leaked, and due to the top blowing off, wild life frequently meandered in and out.

Inside was even worse. Used as storage, the elements of nature had destroyed everything. The worst part? It was not our shed. It was our neighbor's and it sat only about 2 feet from our property line with the door facing our front porch.

I was constantly torn between being thankful for our incredible view or embarrassed by the eye sore that greeted our visitors. I caught myself explaining this dilemma to our then 6-month old son. My conversation went something like this:

"Do you see that shed? That is not our shed. It's our neighbor's. It looks horrid. Maybe someday it will become weak enough to push over. Maybe someday it will spontaneously explode, and I will have a piece of property that doesn't humiliate your mama."

As I have reflected on that conversation, which was ripe with sarcasm, disgust, and disdain I have been saddened by the lack of thanksgiving I was teaching our son.

A spirit of thanksgiving does not start when a child understands what thankfulness means. Teaching thankfulness starts in the womb as the child responds and feels what is communicated through the mothers neurohormones. Research indicates quite firmly that a mother's emotions effects their unborn babies. It's absolutely incredible!

You know the old saying, *"Momma ain't happy, ain't nobody happy."* It is sadly true. As the heart of the home, mothers typically set the emotional tone of the house. Do we have bad days? Um, yeah. Can I get an amen on that one? We have bad days. We have sinful days. Just like anybody we have days in which we completely fail at being the heart and healers of our home.

However, the Bible does not tell us to only be grateful on the good days.

Oh, give thanks to the Lord, for He is good! I Chronicles 16:34.

We are thankful because the Lord is good! I can choose thanksgiving not because of my circumstances, attitude, or my own 'goodness,' but because of the graciousness, love, and forgiveness of a perfect and holy God.

I can be thankful because of a God who forgives through the working and power of Jesus Christ (John 3:36). Every thankful byproduct of our heart should stem from the truth that a perfect and holy God set us free from a life of sin and condemnation.

What freedom that gives me!

Day 5
<u>Therapeia</u>

But the crowds learned about it and followed him. He welcomed them and spoke to them about the kingdom of God, and healed those who needed healing.
Luke 9:11 ESV

The Lord answered, "Who then is the faithful and wise manager, whom the master puts in charge of his servants to give them their food allowance at the proper time?
Luke 12:42 ESV

Down the middle of the great street of the city. On each side of the river stood the tree of life, bearing twelve crops of fruit, yielding its fruit every month. And the leaves of the tree are for the healing of the nations.
Revelation 22:2 NIV

I pushed my stroller down the street as I listened to yet another podcast on my daily walk. These were my times of refreshment, my times to refocus, my times to heal. I loved these times.

The podcast that day was talking about a word that puzzled me. The word was 'therapeia'. The speakers were talking about how mothers could become healers in their homes. I chucked to myself and thought, *'this is getting a little too wacka-doodle for me.'* I almost turned the podcast off. But then they opened to scripture and my interest was peeked.

We are going to get a little technical here now, so hang on to your hats! I promise that it will be worth understanding this little word.

The Greek word for household in these passages is the word 'therapeia.' The word is a noun and the part of speech is feminine. If you go to Strong's Concordance the short definition is 'care, attention, healing.' It is traditionally where we get the word therapeutic from.

The scriptures only use the feminine version of this word 3 times. The first is in Luke 9:11, and refers to Jesus healing all who needs healing. The second in Luke 12:42, and it denotes the people of the home. The final use is in Revelations 2:22, and get this, this final reference describes the tree of life and how its fruit heals the nations of the world. Am I going too far by thinking that those three references are no coincidence? Oh, the astounding truth of God's holy word.

Let us go back to Luke 12:42. In this case the word therapeia refers to the home or household. Wait a second, did you just see the connection there? It's subtle and a little out of context, but I think there is a beautiful truth in that little word. Our homes are meant to be places of healing.

Now it is important to note before I continue that I believe the context of a specific verse should be applied based on what surrounds the given passage. The verses surrounding this passage are going a completely different direction than biblical homemaking.

However, the Bible has truth that continually seeps from its pages. It oozes from the smallest of words to the largest of Gospel truths.

Our homes are to be a place of healing. A healing place for our entire family. Spiritually healing, mentally healing, physically healing. How can we support a healing environment as mothers? Mothers are typically the managers of our household. Not always, but especially in the Christian culture, mothers tend to own that role.

Obviously, we are not always medical healers. But remember the first use of the word in Luke 9:11 refers to Jesus' healing. Jesus didn't just heal medically. He healed body, mind, and soul. What would happen to our homes if we turned it into a place of healing? A place of rejuvenation? A place of wholesome learning? A place of joy? A place of laughter? A place of worship?

The Bible tells us that,

The wisest of women builds her house, but folly with her own hands tears it down. Proverbs 14:1 ESV.

The building of a healing home starts with the mother. We are on the front lines of building up or tearing down our homes. That is quite a responsibility. It's a responsibility that we should and can wear proudly because that is how God has *made us!* We will be most satisfied when we are most satisfied in God and how he designed and created us.

I heard a quote once that the father is the head of the home, the mother the heart of the home, and the children the hope of the home. The Bible tells us that from the heart flows the springs of life (Proverbs 4:23). Practically speaking the heart is what pumps the lifeblood to all other parts of the body.

Are you surrendering today and building your home up, or tearing it down?

When Mama is Scared

"This, then, is how you should pray: "'Our Father in heaven,
hallowed be your name, your kingdom come, your will be done,
on earth as it is in heaven. Give us today our daily bread.
Matthew 6:9-11 NIV

I was scared. Not just a little scared, but a lot scared.

Everything in my life was seemingly falling apart. I was 7 months pregnant, in counseling, God seemed distant, and inside I felt like I was dying inside. I hated every part of being pregnant. The baby would kick and I felt nothing. No joy, no anticipation, no love. Deep inside I feared that I hated my child. I despised my feelings, but it was as if my emotions were locked inside and I didn't have the key.

They laid that baby on my chest a couple months later and I still felt nothing. *Dear Jesus, help me!* That was the moment I was most afraid. I was suddenly the mother of a ten pound 6- ounce baby and I wanted to feel something, but I all I felt was darkness. Yet God heard my plea.

I tell people that I had the opposite of post partum depression. I had pregnancy depression. Within 24 hours of my first born baby being born the fog that had settled over my mind, heart, and soul started to life. It was a turning point.

God had heard me, and an amazing journey of restoration and healing was about to being.

How about you? Most mamas that I talk to have some sort of story. Some sort of "I was here, and then God took me there."

Do you have a turning point in your motherhood journey? Think back to it. Chances are, all our stories have one very key element in common. Surrender.

Our stories merge at the surrender point. Our parenting, mothering, and life merge at the sweet point of surrender.

Mama your life is stressful. It is abundantly clear that our world continues to operate under the assumption that mama's can do it all. Our stress and worry levels are sky high and we often don't know where to turn.

Why is it so tough to trust God? Why can we not surrender our heart, mind, and soul to an all powerful omnipotent creator? Why do you think Jesus told us to pray for our 'daily' bread? Why not monthly, weekly, bi-weekly? Do you think it's perhaps because He knew we would need the daily reminder of Him?

Mama, we need more Jesus in our life every single day. Rely on him when the fear strikes. Rely on him more and more.

Day 7
<u>A Healing Home</u>

Submit yourselves, then, to God.
Resist the devil, and he will flee from you.
James 4:7 NIV

I sat in my living room sobbing. My husband sat across from me. Our kids played on the floor. We were trying to keep our voice and tones reasonable, but I knew we were getting close to our voices raised.

My two year old came over to me, *"It is okay Mama, you don't need to cry."* I started to sob even harder. This wasn't a healing home. This wasn't what God had planned for my family. What was I going to do?

Surrender.

Have you noticed a theme throughout these last 7 days. I hope you have noticed that word *surrender* quite a few times. I used to think that creating a healing home started with myself. I used to think that our healing home had to be perfect. It does not. I used to think that I was a failure on the days that it didn't all to according to plan.

Those just might be the days the most healing occurs.

Today I want you to write down your own version of what a 'healing home' looks like. Literally! Take a moment and write down what your definition of a healing home is.

What does it say? Read it out loud.

I will go next.

My healing home is a place that Jesus reigns supreme. It's a place that no matter what happens in this world my children and husband can step inside and feel a calming peace wash over them. It's ultimately not because of anything I have built. It feels like a healing home because God has created a place that there is unity, prayer, and peace.

Yet, what happens when it does not feel healing? That is the beauty of the Gospel of Jesus Christ. It is not about feelings. It is about surrender, trust, and hope.

You are not going to be a perfect mom or wife. Your husband is not going to be a perfect father and spouse. There will be days where tensions rise. There will be turmoil and a sense of hopelessness, but that is when the Gospel can rise up in your life and transform your home.

Submit yourself to God. This is when powerful transformation can occur in the moments that seem worrisome and hopeless.

"Anxiety in a man's heart weighs him down, but a good word makes him glad."

Proverbs 12:25 ESV

Day 8

<u>*We Don't Know What to Do*</u>

"We don't know what to do, but our eyes are on you!"
2 Chronicles 20:12 ESV

I recently discovered a verse that has transformed the way I look at life. Yes, literally transformed. There is consistent power of scripture to revolutionize perspectives in life. A book of the Bible that has been read a dozen times suddenly unravels a new previously unseen truth. There is great power in the Scriptures of the Almighty God. In this case, a passage shifted my perspective simply with the acknowledgement of how little I know.

"We don't know what to do, but our eyes are on you!"

The statement was a cry out to God by King Jehoshaphat on the cusp of a great battle. He declared earlier in the verse that Judah was *powerless against this great horde that is coming against us'* (1 Chronicles 20:12).

Powerless. Sound familiar? We as Mama's often feel powerless. When our kid is crying and we have no idea why. When they are throwing a tantrum and we are already exhausted mentally and physically. When worry or anxiety hits like a tilde wave. When the budget is tight, but you need diapers. When a pandemic hits (2020 flashback anyone?) and everyone's life changes.

Our eyes are on you Jesus. That is all we can do.

King Jehoshaphat was afraid, he was terribly afraid (vs 3), and yet he still had enough sense to proclaim a fast across Judah (vs 3), cry out to God (vs 5-12), and worship (vs 18). In fact, King Jehoshaphat had people singing and worshiping the Lord go before the army into battle. Can you imagine?! A worship team going before the army.

We do not know what to do, but our eyes are on you. The more I hear that verse the more powerful it seems. It is a complete acknowledgement that we are clueless in our knowledge, but God is sovereign. In that humility there is strength. King Jehoshaphat humbled himself and in that strength he won a great battle.

When you humble yourself before God, victories you never thought possible can suddenly become possible. Worries that seemed deep as the ocean, suddenly calm inside your heart.

The entire nation of Judah humbled themselves before the Lord. Mama worries are a real thing. We all have them and we all at some point feel helpless, but that is the perfect time to put your eyes back on Jesus.

If only we would turn *"Our eyes are on you,"* we would see great things.

Day 9
<u>Weighing Down</u>

"Anxiety in a man's heart weighs him down, but a good word makes
him glad."
Proverbs 12:25 ESV

There was a time in my life that I was not a mother. It was a simpler time. Wink Wink. There was not as much laundry. It didn't matter if my husband and I ate whatever was in the fridge, and watched movies for the next 4 hours.

But what strikes me most is that there was not as much worry in my heart. My heart is so much more sensitive to pain and death. When my babies are running around in our safe little haven, it seems as if the world will never touch them. Yet other times thoughts invade my heart and my children become delicate, helpless, and my perceived ability to protect them is shaken.

God says a lot about worry. It is interesting that he knows us so well to pack his Word with beautiful truths to impact our soul. Proverbs 12:25 tells us,

"Anxiety in a man's heart weighs him down, but a good word makes him glad."

As Christians we have our Savior, Jesus Christ, who our full anxiety can be cast upon. He cares for us in deeper ways than we can possibly understand. He died for us!

As a mother, I desire that my children tell me their burdens. That they trust me enough to cast their worries on me. How much more does our heavenly father, who cares for us perfectly, want us to bask in his love as we turn to him?

Cast all your anxiety on him because he cares for you.
1 Peter 5:7

We all wish there was a magic formula for giving our anxiety to God, but there is not. One thing we do know is that we continually need to be giving over our anxiety to God by prayer and petition.

Why give our anxiety to God? The answer is simple, because he cares for us and has the power to transform our mind and heart. Cast your anxiety on him because not only does he care, **but he can take it away.**

There is still no magical formula for turning our anxieties over to God. For some of us the process may be easy. For others casting our anxieties over to God is a life long process. Jesus gives peace unlike that of the world. His peace is perfect and good. The world is tainted by sin and no perfect peace is found. Jesus can give you beautiful and perfect peace (John 14:27).

Day 10
<u>*Let's Get Practical*</u>

Finally, brothers and sisters, whatever is true, whatever is noble, whatever is right, whatever is pure, whatever is lovely, whatever is admirable—if anything is excellent or praiseworthy—think about such things.
Philippians 4:8 NIV

I was driving down the road with my baby and two year old. It was a cold winter day and all in all it wasn't that bad of a morning! Mom win, am I right!? As I drove down a Minnesota road that I had driven hundreds of times a semi drove toward me in the opposite lane.

As the semi came closer, without warning, without permission from my heart or mind, a picture of my baby suddenly being thrown onto the road and underneath that semi hit my mind unwelcomed and unannounced.

I gripped the steering wheel harder. Where had that thought came from? I could not get the picture out of my head. Tears started to fill my eyes, my heart started to tighten, it felt hard to breath.

This was just one of many unwelcomed and unannounced images that have hit my mind since having my second child. They come at me as I drive. The images immediately produce fear unlike any I have previously experienced. My whole body feels heavy and tried as I fight the unwelcomed intrusion into my mothering.

Anxiety can wear you down, it can literally weigh you down! Take a peek back at Proverbs 12:25 from yesterday. And what cheers the heart back up? A kind word. Think about that with me. What is a kind word? Is it someone speaking to you kindly? Maybe, but I have a tendency to believe that we need to seek out our kind words.

It means surrounding ourselves with Bible believers, reading our Bible, listening to a podcast or sermon, and practicing what is **good, honorable, and lovely** (Philippians 4:8).

Let us get practical. It's not as easy to overcome fear by just believing the truth. Our hearts still stumble, our emotions and hormones are still ever present. God has given those emotions and hormones to us for a reason. But basking in them, letting them sink in and take rest, will not aid you.

How do we overcome worry in practical ways?

Read Our Bibles

God's Word is here for a reason. It is meant to teach and train us in our walk with God. Memorize it's truths, because when the worry sets in, God's truth is our light to combat our untruth.

Memorize Scripture

Memorize God's words as worry is vanquished. Peter 3:12 reminds us that God hears our prayers. Lift your worries to him. Memorizing scripture can be our powerful weapon when anxiety hits.

I have hidden your word in my heart that I might not sin against you. Psalm 119:11 NIV

Worship

One of the most powerful ways to bring our focus and affections back to God is to worship. Worship matters and we can find rest and rejuvenation by declaring in song the wonders of our God.

Take these practical steps and see what God can do to calm your anxious and worrisome mama heart.

Day 11
<u>Change</u>

When I am afraid, I put my trust in you. In God, whose word I praise
—in God I trust and am not afraid.
What can mere mortals do to me?
Psalm 56:3-4 NIV

Edited from original 2019 writing

Something has been happening lately, and it has been leaving me unraveled, scared, and a bit crazy. Change. I am left with this phrase scrambling in my head, "how to embrace change?"

Change is everywhere.

My body is changing, the number of children I have will soon change, a possible c-section is looming in my near future, we are making plans to put our home on the market, I am driving a different car, our routine is changing , and finally my career is changing. That last one continues to have my heart skip a beat, my stomach lurch, and my head spin.

Here is the truth that I am trying my hardest not to talk about.

I am not okay.

Sometimes God stretches us in ways that we do not anticipate. A career change, a possible c-section, additional children, moving, new cars, financial stresses, new routines, and our mind and heart seem to be spinning out of control. How to embrace change when this happens is not easy.

How do we embrace change in a godly way when our mind and heart are spinning out of control?

I will be honest, I do not like where God is currently leading. I would much rather have control and pursue the things that I want. Like some crazy control psychopath, I have a sinful wish to control the circumstances I wish to change. That desire is rooted in something just as sinful called fear.

There is a book that has aided me greatly over the years. Kimberly Wagner writes about the power of a soft warrior through her book *Fierce Women*. In the book she explains two types of fierce women. The first is a fierce woman that demands power. This woman is fierce, passionate, beautiful, and will tear the walls down to accomplish what she wants. Meeting the world head on, nothing will stop her. She is fierce, but it is not a beautiful fierceness. It is a sinful fierceness.

The second is still a fierce woman, but there are some real differences. Instead of using her fierceness to tear down in the process of accomplishing what she wants, she instead builds up. She is soft, generous, passionate, secure, loving; and yet she still is a powerhouse of strength and integrity. Her fierceness is beautiful because it is rooted in her Savior Jesus.

A fierce, strong, beautiful women cannot co-exist with an anxious heart. But why? Anxiety and fear cannot coexists with a fierce woman that is rooted in our Savior Jesus. Root ourselves in Jesus and unashamedly reject anxiety.

Day 12
<u>The Sanctification of a Messy House</u>

Peace I leave with you; my peace I give you. I do not give to you as the world gives. Do not let your hearts be troubled and do not be afraid.
John 14:27 NIV

The house was a mess and I was at my wits end. The messier the house got, the more spills, and the crazier the children acted the more the pit of my stomach was turning into a knot. Sadly, this was not an isolated incident, it happens quite regularly.

Mama you are strong! Most days we can take on whatever is thrown at us head on. There are other days when our resolve is weakened and our peace can get crushed by something as simple as a messy home.

One of the things that Jesus has used to lead me to a more sanctified life is my messy house. I like my home clean, neat, and organized. There is not one of those things that are more important than the next. I want all of them at all times. That has become an idol of unrest in my heart.

Kids are messy and the mess is beautiful. Often messes mean kids are learning! So how does the beauty of a learning child meet with my idol of organization and cleanliness? Truthfully it does not.

As believers in Jesus Christ we no longer live in the ways of this world. As funny as it sounds, that includes living in a messy house! Christ is the one who lives in us. We have the choice to let our messy house drive us toward Christ or let our sinful heart drive us further away from Christ.

Does that mean that our anxious thoughts or feelings will just vanish? Does it mean that my frustrations when I have a messy house will vanish? We live in a sinful world where burdens are daily apart of our sanctification. But stick with me for a moment, our sanctification is beautiful. We daily struggle, fight, and skirmish, not for glory in this world, but the paradise that is awaiting us in the beautiful arms of our savior.

Waiting is hard, but in the waiting, there is beautiful hope for our lives. What we do in that waiting is key. Mama, let your heart feel the anxiety and frustration, but instead of letting those feelings turn sinful, let God's sanctification draw you more near to your Savior Jesus.

Day 13
<u>A Heavy Potato</u>

Love the Lord your God with all your heart and with all your soul
and with all your strength.
Deuteronomy 6:5

I love potatoes. Mashed potatoes, twice baked potatoes, baked potatoes, Texas potatoes, purple potatoes, russet potatoes, golden potatoes, red potatoes; you get the idea. Give me any sort of potatoes, especially during pregnancy, and I will gobble them up. Yet if I eat them every day, I will pack on the pounds. They are high in carbohydrates and sugar. Even though there are beautiful nutrients in them, I can easily over indulge.

There are things in life that are similar. Those things that are good, but if consumed on a regular basis, they will weigh us down just like eating potatoes every day may not be good for most people.

What happens when the good things of life become our primary objective? When eating healthy takes away the joy of consuming food. Or preparing healthy dishes takes away valuable time from our families? When exercise becomes obsessive instead of constructive? When cloth diapering becomes a pride issue instead of a helpful habit? When reading your Bible is a checklist item instead of an intimate experience with your Savior. There are many scenarios that could turn into 'primary' objectives instead of a healing or helpful lifestyle.

Do you see where I'm going with this?

I am sure you do because there has been countless sermons, devotionals, and books written on the topic of replacing the good things with the best thing.

The best thing on this earth is when our affections and heart are turned toward Jesus in every way.

Easier said than done when our habits weigh us down more than they aid us in turning our hearts back to Jesus. Maybe that is how we evaluate if a habit is worth our time. Is it consuming our hearts with heaviness by it's disciple? Or is it turning our affections back toward Christ?

Start evaluating your habits. Take time to read scripture instead of rushing to make make the healthiest breakfast possible. Play with your children instead of obsessing over the cloth diaper stash. Go on a nature walk with your family and bask in the creation of God instead of cranking out a harsh three miles at the gym.

It is about our heart. It is about the choices we make that turn our affections toward God instead of toward our worrisome self.

Anxiety in a man's heart weighs him down, but a good word makes him glad. Proverbs 12:25.

Day 14
Gratitude,
an Antidote for Worry

Rejoice always! Pray constantly. Give thanks in everything, for this is
God's will for you in Christ Jesus.
Thessalonians 5:16–18

Not too long ago my toddler learned to say sorry and please. He
seems to be a repeating robot as he utilizes his newly acquired
manners. Yet the phrase 'thank you' has been just as prevalent of
teaching as the other two phrases, and yet he has resisted putting
those words into practice.

Want to worry less? Practice gratitude? Want less fear in your life?
Practice gratitude. Want more joy in your life? Practice gratitude.

Thanksgiving is simply the acknowledge of the goodness of God in
our daily life. As far as I can tell, the bible never gives us an exact
formula for expressing gratitude, it simply says to do it.

Even Jesus gave thanks in many ways to his Father, including for
his provision (Matthew 15:36) and for being heard by his father
(John 11:41–43).

Yet, he also explicitly states that the Father knows what we are
going to say before we even say it (Matthew 6:7–8), so why show
gratitude when God already knows our heart? God specifically tells
us that it is his will for us to be grateful and thankful.

Science continues to back up what the Bible and God has already been saying. Isn't that incredible?! Practicing gratitude on a daily basis is not only good for us spiritually, but also physically!

Robert Emmons is a leading expert on the science of gratitude, and even he has found that gratitude has unending benefits for our health. Feelings of gratitude can increase our immune system, lower blood pressure, and give deeper sleep!

Turn your heart and mind toward gratitude and see if it becomes your antidote for anxiety.

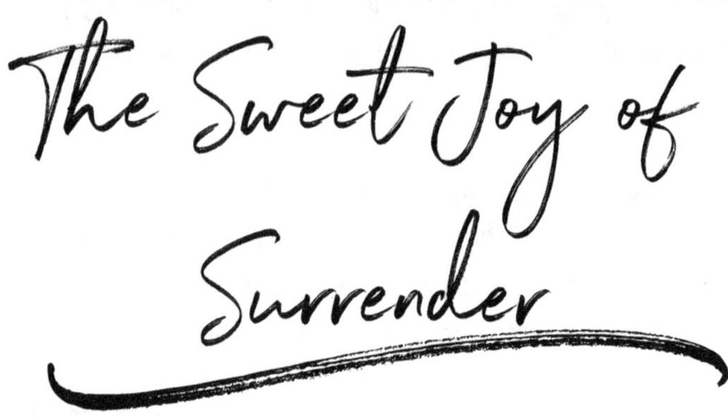

But the fruit of the Spirit is love, joy, peace, patience, kindness, goodness, faithfulness, gentleness, self-control; against such things there is no law.
Galatians 5:22-23 ESV

Day 15

Being a godly Mother in an ungodly World

But the fruit of the Spirit is love, joy, peace, patience, kindness, goodness, faithfulness, gentleness, self-control; against such things there is no law.
Galatians 5:22-23 ESV

Have you watched the popular Disney movie "Tangled"? In it a demented mother Gothel impressively sings her heart out to the show stopper song, "Mother Knows Best." The song spins a tale of how Gothel knows exactly what is best for her captive daughter. Gothel is a picturesque representation of the selfishness that runs rampant in this sinful world. She is about as ungodly as it comes.

Yet what I find so fascinating is that this culture often strives for the very things that made Mother Gothel disgusting. Mother Gothel's entirety could be summarized by "a selfish pursuit of oneself." Yet that is exactly what is praised in the world's definition of a good mother. The world preaches putting ourselves first. The bible says differently.

How do we be a godly mother in an ungodly world?

Motherhood is the ministry of glorifying God through nurturing the hearts of our families. Gloria Flurman in her book, calls this *Missional Motherhood.* Nurturing does not just belong to the biological mothers, it belongs to all women.

We are all daughters of Eve and by extension all have mothering or nurturing instincts. We were made for nurturing the world. When we look at motherhood as a ministry it becomes a trajectory of sharing the gospel with our families and everyone around us. Yet, the biblical role of a mother is very purposeful. She has Christlike qualities that flow out through the fruits of the spirit.

The preoccupation with self is a destroyer of the home. So often we are busy building ourselves up, promoting self, building our careers, engaging in self-care, creating a beautiful home, or any number of high callings that we forget our greatest calling.

Our greatest calling as believers in Jesus Christ is to pursue Jesus and bring glory to God. Bringing glory to someone besides ourselves is in direct conflict with the world's determination to pursue the best version of ourselves. Yet, God calls us to bring glory to him through every part of our lives, including motherhood.

Being a godly mother in an ungodly world is not easy because this world is not perfect. We are waiting for our perfect Savior to redeem this broken and ungodly world. This world is not our home, but while we are in it, learning godliness in motherhood can impact the world.

Day 16

<u>Characteristics of a Godly Mother</u>

You shall therefore lay up these words of mine in your heart and in your soul, and you shall bind them as a sign on your hand, and they shall be as frontlets between your eyes. You shall teach them to your children, talking of them when you are sitting in your house, and when you are walking by the way, and when you lie down, and when you rise.
Deuteronomy 11:18-19 ESV

I starred at the diapers in my hand. They felt like a symbol of my failure. It was 2020, and I was working more and seeing my children less. My world had gone topsy turvy and the things that once were a priority were shifting to accommodate the dysfunction of a dysfunctional time.

The diapers in my hands were cloth diapers and they were a symbol of being a 'good' mother in my heart. I knew that I had to let them go. I just didn't have time to clean, fold, and maintain the cute little fluff butts that my children roamed the earth in.

It was killing me inside to order disposable diapers. You might think I was crazy, but it was one of the last expectations I had for myself as a young mom that God was stripping away to teach me surrender.

It is interesting the pressures that we put on ourselves. When I step into eternity, I don't imagine that cloth diapering my sons will mean anything in the grand design of this life. Yet I held so dearly to my cloth diapering standard that when it was being taken from me, I felt like a failure.

What if instead of measuring ourselves against the world, or our standards, we started measuring ourselves against scripture? What will we find there?

The characteristics of a godly mother:

**A godly mother will pursue the Gospel first.
(1 Corinthians 15:2-3)**

**A godly mother Will Treasure the Word of God.
(Deuteronomy 11:18-21)**

**A godly mother will find contentment in Christ.
(Psalm 38:9)**

**A godly mother will discipline herself in the faith.
(1 Timothy 4:7-8)**

**A godly mother will love her husband well.
(Genesis 2:18)**

We will never be perfect moms, but we can be in pursuit of godly qualities that lead us to be a good mom in pursuit of a perfect Savior.

Day 17
The Interruptions of Motherhood

Overhearing what they said, Jesus told him, "Don't
be afraid; just believe."
Mark 5:36 NIV

Are there other mamas out there that experience constant
interruptions by their kids? Not only are we busy as moms,
but there are continual interruptions. It never seems to
stop! Just when one kid does not need our full attention,
the next one is ready with another need.

If I did not know better, I would say they are holding
secret meetings in the morning. At these meetings they
carefully map out the interruption agenda for the day. The
first one decides to be the interrupter from 8am-9:45am,
and the next one is on interrupter duty from 9:45am-
10:30am. And so on and so forth. It's enough to make any
mom go mad!

Take a moment and read Mark 5:21-43.

Interruptions by our children are not necessarily a bad
thing. Some of the greatest Jesus stories in the Bible start
with Jesus being interrupted. Sometimes his interruption
was interrupted! Miracles were performed because
someone had the audacity to interrupt Jesus from his task.

The ministry of motherhood is often similar. As the interruptions of our children surmount, they often can lead to greater things that we do not expect.

Did you read through mark 5:21:43? How many interruptions did you count? I count at least three. One of my favorites sentences of this text is from verse 35, *"While Jesus was still speaking..."* Sound familiar? How many times a day are you interrupted by your children while you are still speaking?!

Ladies, dare I say it? Jesus knows what it is like to be a mother with constant interruptions. He was interrupted before he even finished talking. A man came to announce that Jairus's had died and there was no need to trouble Jesus any longer. I don't know about you ladies, but if someone came to me in the middle of my day and told me that I didn't have to take care of something an interruption had caused, I would thank them and cross it off my to-do list without hesitation.

Not Jesus. Thankfully we have a perfect Savior that doesn't hesitate to do the right thing. All the interruptions in Mark 5 are about to lead to a divine miracle. A women that had bleeding for 12 years touched Jesus and was healed.

Jesus had already been interrupted, and yet this women interruptions his mission yet again. Can you relate? Have you been interrupted time and time again by your children's constant touching? You may not be able to heal them like Jesus, but you also have a healing touch that only you as their mother can give. Maybe they need a hug, a high five, a moment of your time to sit with them.

Those ministry of motherhood moments can be life-giving to children and all it takes is their interruption to become your moment to minister.

Don't underestimate the interruptions in your mothering. You never know when a interruptions is going to lead to a divine moment that only God could orchestrate.

Jesus knows our struggles, even the interruptions that drive us nuts. We see this in Mark 5 as Jesus was interrupted time and time again, yet these divine interruptions led to divine miracles. Motherhood is the ministry of interruptions. It is laying down our needs in the moment and attending to the needs of another, but doing it with grace. Allow the interruptions to drive you to Jesus.

Showing Kindness Daily

*"Dear children, let's not merely say that we
love each other; let us show the truth by our actions."*
1 John 3:18 (ESV)

Kindness. An intrinsic reaction of showing gratitude and generosity to those around us.

Recent events of my life have left me at considering the above definition of kindness. Kindness used to be something I took for granted. In my little conservative Christian bubble, I had not been exposed to unkindness on a daily level. It was common to experience the unkindness of circumstances and society, but the unkindness of Christianity has crept into my life over the last year and truly shook my foundation.

I was struck with a question from someone recently that left me quite sad. A very unkind situation was unraveling, and my heart was grieved. When I asked that person what Jesus would have done, this statement was shot back at me, *"Jesus would have been the one fighting at the front."*

Let me be clear, the situation was unkind. There was gossip, revenge, back stabbing, and very little room for debate on the fact that the situation was taking a sinful turn.

I'm not going to dive into the theological ocean of what Jesus would do if he were in any of the unkind or unjust situations, we find ourselves in. That theological rabbit trail is left to better theologians than me.

However, Jesus told us to follow him. To continue the work, he had done on this earth. To be a city on a hill that cannot be hidden. To lay down our lives and follow him. Jesus laid down his life and sacrificed it for us. What better way to follow than to lay down our selfishness and follow his example?

Our words and actions have meaning, they are charged by our heart. Is your heart actions fueled by the cross of Jesus Christ or the cross of selfish death? It's time to fuel your heart with surrender and turn to kindness.

Your words and actions are going to directly teach your children how to act in this world. Will you show them Jesus or the world today?

Day 19
<u>Weighing your Heart</u>

All deeds are right in the sight of the doer,
but the Lord weighs the heart.
Proverbs 21:12 (ESV)

I watched as the world went to pot in 2020. Did you just chuckle when you read that sentence? My guess is that you at the very least emphasized with it. Many of us watched the world in complete disbelief in 2020. Yet, it should not surprise us because the Bible is clear that the world is going to become more and more ugly as His coming draws near (2 Timothy 3:1-4).

Our hearts want vindication for the injustice of this world. To assume that the people around us are wrong and we are right. We know the truth of the gospel, but do not mistake the truth as an excuse for unkindness. Jesus never did. He knew more about truth than anyone that has ever stepped foot on this earth. Yet most of his ministry was rooted in kindness and love toward ALL of mankind.

So where does that leave us? How do we balance justice and love in a world that is full of injustice, hatred, and falsehood? I personally believe the balance is united at kindness. Teaching kindness should begin in the home and then extend into the world. We are the hands and feet of Jesus (1 Corinthians 12:27).

Little children cry when their toys break because they know intrinsically that brokenness is wrong. Yet we teach our children not to throw the toy in anger, but to work through the emotions that plague their little hearts with compassion and love. We might help them repair the toy, or even buy a new one, but most of our energy is not focused on fixing the problem as much as it is guiding our children in how to work through the disappointment of brokenness in a constructive manner.

Think of the gospel for a moment. God created the world, man, and women and declared everything good. Sin entered the world and humans embraced it. We rejected God and turned away from truth. Yet God continued to pursue us. Jesus, God himself, came to earth and ministered to the poor and rich alike.

Then the greatest unkindness seen in human history unraveled. Jesus was brutally tortured and killed by those same people he was coming to save. Our little selfish feelings are grains of sand in compression to the unkindness and injustice done to our Savior. It seems frail to say that an unkindness was done to Jesus. The entire wrath of God was poured out on him.

The unkindness that we feel in this world is nothing in comparison (Galatians 3:13). Yet such a ravage act of unkindness led to the greatest gift for you and me; our salvation. Jesus arose from the dead and extends grace and mercy every day to the same mankind that rejects what he offers with every dark deed of selfish pursuit.

Day 20
<u>*Living Abundantly*</u>

The thief comes only to steal and kill and destroy.
I came that they may have life and have it abundantly.
John 10:10 (ESV)

I sat on the floor playing *Paw Patrol* for the millionth time with my 2-year old. My heart was full. I felt like this was 'the life'. The life I had wanted, but did not know I wanted. Isn't Jesus good? Even through all the trials and discomforts of motherhood, we still have our cup overflowing with his blessings.

My cup is always overflowing. It overflows when the blessings in my life are more than my cup can hold. Does that sound too good to be true? I have news for you. Your cup already overflows too. If you have placed your trust in Christ Jesus, then your cup is overflowing and spilling out with abundance. In Christ, we have overflowing joy, overflowing love, overflowing abundance, and more.

Living in God's abundance starts with the grace of Jesus Christ coming into our lives. As we are sanctified and grow in Him, he gives us a blessing of good things. That abundance should produce in us a desire to bring Him more glory.

Seek the Kingdom of God above all else, and live righteously, and he will give you everything you need. Matthew 6:33 NLT

Ladies, motherhood can be hard. Creating a healing and hopeful home for your family to grow up in can seem like an insurmountable task. But you have been given abundance in Christ.

Many of us have a tendency to think that everything in this life should be handed to us, including our abundant life. However, read Matthew 6:33 again. Notice something key, what proceeds God giving you everything you need?

We are called to live righteously and seek God's kingdom. The price of salvation comes with no strings attached, but submitting to God's Word will produce in us a desire to follow him correctly and passionately. Our affections and desires will turn toward our Savior on a daily and hourly basis.

Your abundant life in Christ begins with submitting to him and then continually living in pursuit of God and his Kingdom.

Day 21
<u>Finding Grace in your</u> <u>Motherhood</u>

But he gives more grace. Therefore it says,
"God opposes the proud, but gives grace to the humble."
James 4:6 ESV

It was falling a part. Everything was falling a part. Nothing was going right and the carefully constructed 'healing home' that I had built was being disassembled before my eyes.

I wanted the doors into my home to feel like a 'healing place,' a 'life-giving place', a place of 'restoration.' Yet instead it felt like a place of death. What could I do?

What I did not understand in the angst and worry of motherhood was that surrender to God's leading needed to be my primary. Sanctification is a painful process, but what we need to understand as mothers is that it is also a healing process.

As we are sanctified through the power of the Holy Spirit to be more like Jesus, our motherhood will go through radical change, radical transformation, and radical construction.

Those things you have built up, may need to be torn down.

My son has two little security blankets. One was knitted by his uncle and it is gorgeous. The other is a fluffy character blanket from his favorite show *Paw Patrol.* He loves them equally. He carries those blankets around like they are a life line. Yet we all know that they are a just a temporary comfort as he grows and changes.

The same can be said about motherhood. We all have security blankets. One of my security blankets is clean floors. When my floors are clean, my entire house seems clean to me. Yet God has taken away my clean floor security blanket more times than I can count and it has been a part of my sanctification process.

Some security blankets are more precious than others. How about time? I used to have a sacred time between 5am-6am to do quiet times with God. There was a season that I felt like a failure when I could not get my babies to go back to bed during that hour. It was just another point of surrender that ultimately led me closer to God instead of further away.

This entire devotional mission has been to take us from a place of desiring that perfect healing home, to a place that we acknowledge the worries, fears, and angst of motherhood, and finally surrender it all to the healing power of God through the sanctification of drawing closer to Jesus.

Do you want a healing home for yourself, your spouse, and your children. Start by surrendering your entire motherhood journey to Jesus. It's at that point that the cultivation of your healing home will begin.

Rachael writes healinghome.co to inspire mama's to pursue Jesus and find beauty, loveliness, healing, health, and inspiration along their own unique journey of creating home.

She is married to a country boy and they live in the back hills of Minnesota with their dog, chickens and two rambunctious little boys.

You can find more about Rachael over on her Instagram page at https://www.instagram.com/healing_home_/

TURN

VACUUM

ON

PUSH
VACUUM